KU-091-512

COFFEE WITH

MARILYN

C O F F E E   W I T H

MARILYN

YONA ZELDIS McDONOUGH

FOREWORD BY GLORIA STEINEM

DUNCAN BAIRD PUBLISHERS

LONDON

Coffee with Marilyn
Yona Zeldis McDonough

First published in the United Kingdom and Ireland in 2007 by
Duncan Baird Publishers Ltd
Sixth Floor, Castle House
75–76 Wells Street, London W1T 3QH

Conceived, created and designed by Duncan Baird Publishers

Managing Editors: Gill Paul and Peggy Vance
Co-ordinating Editors: Daphne Razazan and James Hodgson
Editor: Jack Tresidder
Assistant Editor: Kirty Topiwala
Managing Designer: Clare Thorpe

British Library Cataloguing-in-Publication Data:
A CIP record for this book is available from the British Library
ISBN: 978-1-84483-466-2
10 9 8 7 6 5 4 3 2 1
Printed in China

Publisher's note:
The interviews in this book are purely fictional, while having a solid basis
in biographical fact. They take place between a fictionalized Marilyn Monroe
and an imaginary interviewer. This literary work has not been approved or
endorsed by Marilyn Monroe's estate.

CONTENTS

Foreword by GLORIA STEINEM

A student, lawyer, teacher, artist, mother, grandmother, defender of animals, rancher, homemaker, sportswoman, rescuer of children— all of these are futures we can imagine for Norma Jeane. If acting had become an expression of that real self, not an escape from it, one also can imagine the whole woman who was both Norma Jeane and Marilyn becoming a serious actress and wise comedienne who would still be working in her sixties, with more productive years to come.

But Norma Jeane remained the frightened child of the past. And Marilyn remained the unthreatening half-person that sex goddesses are supposed to be.

It is the lost possibilities of Marilyn Monroe that capture our imaginations. It was the lost

Norma Jeane, looking out of Marilyn's eyes, who captured our hearts.

Now that more women are declaring our full humanity—now that we are more likely to be valued for our heads and hearts, not just the bodies that house them—we also wonder: Could we have helped Marilyn survive?

There can be no answer.

But most of us, men as well as women, are trying to bridge some distance between our uniqueness and what the world rewards. If we learn from the life of Marilyn Monroe, she will live on in us.

INTRODUCTION

Marilyn Monroe's story reads like a fairy tale
of wishes fulfilled and unfulfilled—a story
quintessentially American yet universal too.
We want to hear it over and over, as if the tale of
her humble beginnings, stunning successes, and
cruel twists of fate really *were* a fairy tale, one
which could return her to us, intact and glowing.

Marilyn's mythic status has become unique. No
other film personality has been written about so
much. None has prompted so much speculation by
biographers and novelists, journalists and conspiracy
theorists. Who was the pretty, smiley-eyed child
who began life as Norma Jeane and whose aura of
innocent sexuality invoked so many fantasies about
her brief and eventually tragic life?

This book is itself a fantasy of a kind—a fiction.

But it is grounded in biographical facts, in interviews she gave, and in the recollections of a wide range of her friends, family, and colleagues. It invites readers to sit down with Marilyn over a coffee and hear her own views on love, sex, films, fame, the life of the body and the life of the mind.

MARILYN MONROE (1926–1962)
Her Life in Short

Marilyn Monroe was born on June 1, 1926, in Los
Angeles General Hospital, the third child of Gladys
Pearl Baker, née Monroe. The birth was an easy one,
even if the life that followed it was not. The child's
birth certificate read "Norma Jeane Mortenson." Her
mother had tried to legalize the birth by using the
surname of her second husband, whom, in fact, she
had left some months before becoming pregnant.
When Norma Jeane was born, Gladys was working
at Consolidated Film Industries as a technician
whose job it was to splice negatives together. Her co-
workers, some of whom she supervised, thought the
baby's father might be another company employee,
but took up a collection to help pay Gladys's hospital
bills. The true identity of Marilyn's father is unknown.

Norma Jeane's early years were spent bouncing around from one foster home to another. Her mother continued to work, and often saw her baby daughter only on weekends. There is a snapshot taken of the two on a rare outing to the beach in 1928: Norma Jeane, blonde and fretful in a striped swimsuit, looks unhappy; her mother, an attractive brunette, seems aloof and guarded. There appears to be little rapport between them and, given the way Norma Jeane's life unspooled, the detachment we see in the photo can be construed as prophetic.

Things were not easy for Gladys, and eventually the strain of her situation broke her. Before Norma Jeane was eight, Gladys suffered a nervous collapse and was hospitalized as a schizophrenic. At the time, Norma Jeane was living with her mother's best friend, whom she lovingly called Aunt Grace. But two years later, when Aunt Grace remarried, her house—and indeed her life—could no longer accommodate Norma Jeane. She packed up all the nine-year-old's things, stowed them in her car, and drove Norma Jeane for a long while without saying where they were going. They arrived at a three-story red-brick building with a sign reading LOS ANGELES ORPHANS' HOME. Norma Jeane broke down and begged Aunt Grace not to leave her at this place. She was not, after all, an orphan: her mother was alive, just temporarily unable to care for her. But Aunt Grace could not be swayed. After promising to return and collect her as soon as she could, she left Norma Jeane at the orphanage.

It took nearly two years for Aunt Grace to make good on her promise—years in which Norma Jeane felt unloved, unwanted, and unworthy in almost every way. She had begun to stammer, and would later say that this began after an incident in which she had been sexually molested in one of her foster homes. The loneliness she had carried with her for years now became a part of her, like her skin or hair.

Norma Jeane left the orphanage just after turning 11, but not to live with Aunt Grace. Instead, she was brought to Aunt Grace's own aunt, Ana Lower, an unmarried 62-year-old who lived in a run-down bungalow in a poor section of Los Angeles. She was wonderfully kind to Norma Jeane, and in return, Norma Jeane loved her with the fullness of her young and still trusting heart.

When Aunt Grace married yet again, she planned to move away from Los Angeles with her new husband. Aunt Ana was considered too old to become the legal guardian of 15-year-old Norma Jeane, so there was once more the problem of what to do with her. The options were yet another foster home or, even worse, a return to the orphanage.

Aunt Grace came up with what she thought was a brilliant solution—Norma Jeane could get married. A neighbor, 21-year-old Jim Dougherty, was thought to be suitable. At first, Norma Jeane protested. She said she was too young to marry and fearful of what a husband might do—or expect from her. Aunt Grace, apparently surprised by Norma Jeane's innocence, assured her that she was young in years only. Aunt Ana bought her a book filled with hints for the bride-to-be. On June 19, 1942, merely weeks after her 16th birthday, Norma Jeane walked down the aisle with Jim. Aunt Ana had designed and made her wedding dress.

Married life didn't turn out to be so bad. Jim was attentive and kind, and seemed happy with Norma Jeane: he told her she was perfect in every way except for her cooking. In 1944 Jim enlisted in the Merchant Marine, went through boot camp, and was sent to

Catalina Island as a physical training instructor. With him went Norma Jeane. Suddenly, her world was teeming with men. Sailors, marines, coastguardsmen were everywhere, and they were not immune to Norma Jeane's ripe allure. Jim was jealous of the wolf whistles and the catcalls. He scolded her about the way she dressed. Norma Jeane was puzzled—what was wrong with the way she dressed? The problem, she decided, was his, not hers.

When Jim was sent to Shanghai, Norma Jeane went back to California to live with his family in Van Nuys, and got a job with the Radio Plane Company in Burbank. She started out as parachute inspector. One day, the Army's Pictorial Center in Hollywood sent photographers into the plant to show workers contributing to the war effort. The moment one of them set eyes on Norma Jeane, he asked if he could take her picture and told her she was "a real morale booster." In the first rolls of film taken, Norma Jeane wore her standard-issue factory overalls. But when the photographer found out she had a sweater in her locker, he wanted to take more pictures of her wearing the sweater instead. His prints appeared in hundreds of Army camp newspapers. Although she didn't know it yet, the course of Norma's Jeane's life had been irrevocably altered.

Those early images sparked the interest of another Army photographer and, eventually, that of a Los Angeles modeling agency boss. Norma Jeane began attending classes at a modeling school attached to this agency, paying the 100-dollar tuition fee out of the money earned from her modeling jobs. Though the head of the agency told her she had "too much sex appeal" to do well as a fashion model, her career blossomed when she began posing in bathing suits. Cheesecake and glamor became the means by which she could leave behind the dreary, workaday world in which she was still an unwanted girl who would never amount to much. She had already started to dream of acting, and believed modeling might be the way to make her dreams come true.

She had a lawyer write to Jim Dougherty, who was still in Shanghai, to say she wanted a divorce. Meanwhile, her career was heating up. Howard Hughes, owner of RKO Studios, asked for a screen test. And Twentieth Century Fox was also looking for fresh faces. It seemed that all at once Norma Jeane had not one but two tantalizing options before her. She met with Fox first. They made a Technicolor test and the next day gave her a stock contract for a year.

It was the Fox studio that rechristened her Marilyn Monroe, a name she liked, especially because it included her mother's maiden name. By this time her wavy, brown hair had gone. She was a blonde—the modeling agency head had seen to that—and an aspiring starlet. At first, there were no movie parts, just endless posing for still shots. There are photographs of her in evening gowns; holding baskets of vegetables and dressed as a farm girl; and wearing a pearl necklace with her blonde tresses upswept. But mostly she posed in bathing suits—one-piece, two-piece, white, peach-colored, striped—offering herself willingly, eagerly, to any audience who wanted to see her.

In 1948, she was finally cast in two pictures, with bit parts in both. *Scudda Hoo! Scudda Hay!* featured the newly-minted Marilyn Monroe rowing a boat; in *Dangerous Years* she played a waitress. Small parts in other forgettable films followed, and her career seemed stalled until she was cast in the 1950 noir classic, *The Asphalt Jungle*. As Angela Phinlay, the mistress of a crooked lawyer involved in a jewel heist,

Monroe began to make people really sit up and take notice. In that same year, she played the nausea-prone Miss Caswell in *All About Eve*. Although it was a small part, she stood out. Marilyn Monroe was already a star in the making.

Films came quickly after that. In 1950 she was cast in *The Fireball*, and played Polly, an enticing roller-skating groupie. Then, *Right Cross* paired her with Dick Powell. She made four films in 1951: *Hometown Story*, *As Young As You Feel*, *Love Nest*, and *Let's Make It Legal*, which starred Claudette Colbert. 1952 was a pivotal year: Marilyn played a fish cannery worker named Peggy in a drama that starred Barbara Stanwyck, Paul Douglas, and Robert Ryan. Although clearly not the lead—that role was reserved for Stanwyck—Monroe brought a fresh quality to the part, and proved that she had a scrappy grace all of her own in the way she portrayed her character's struggle to accept what life and love have to offer. That same year she appeared in *We're Not Married*, *Monkey Business*, *O. Henry's Full House*, and *Don't Bother to Knock*. In the last of these she was cast, against type, as Nell, a psychotic young babysitter.

In 1953 she played the more substantial part of Rose Loomis, an adulterous and murderous wife, in *Niagara*. This featured the long hip-swinging walk that became part of her legend. In the same year, she and Jane Russell co-starred in the musical comedy, *Gentlemen Prefer Blondes*, a film that both established her as a superstar and defined her "Marilyn" persona as a wide-eyed, unconsciously humorous sex-bombshell. Her funny and sharp portrayal of the showgirl Lorelei Lee introduced a whispery voice, soon to be mistaken for her normal one.

"Young lady, do you mean to tell me you don't want to marry my son for his money?" thunders

Tommy Noonan's outraged father when he learns that his son has fallen in love with a woman he considers nothing but a cold-hearted gold digger. "No," she replies, all sweetness and indignation. "I want to marry him for *your* money!" The father, astonished by her honesty and wit, is eventually charmed and the film ends, as such comedies inevitably do, in a double wedding.

This triumph was followed by a reprise of the "dumb blonde" in *How to Marry a Millionaire*, in which she co-starred with Betty Grable and Lauren Bacall. Both roles allowed Monroe's gifts as a comedic actress to shine, and would later pave the way for what many consider her best film, Billy Wilder's inimitable gender-bending comedy, *Some Like It Hot* (1959).

Wilder cast her as Sugar Kane, a ukulele-toting singer who is tired of "getting the fuzzy end of the lollipop" and finally finds love and happiness with the cross-dressing saxophonist played by Tony Curtis. It's a fast-paced, brilliant comedy, totally improbable yet utterly hilarious, and Monroe's buoyant flesh and achingly sweet expression—filmed in black and white—are the scaffolding on which its antic humor is precisely and delicately balanced.

Between *Gentlemen Prefer Blondes* and *Some Like It Hot* were other starring roles, like a saloon singer in *River of No Return* (1954); Vicky, a nightclub singer, in *There's No Business Like Show Business* (1954); and the leading lady in *The Seven Year Itch*, shot the same year. A publicity shot for this film produced perhaps the most famous image in cinema history—Marilyn laughing with joy as the wind from a New York subway grating blows her white skirt skyward.

After making this film, fed up with the roles she was being offered, Monroe fled Hollywood and went to New York City to study with the Method director Lee Strasberg at his Actors Studio. Though she learned a great deal, the emphasis on a cerebral approach to acting was unsuited to her special talents, and Fox soon lured her back with the new and better contract she had been demanding. Her performance in Joshua Logan's 1956 *Bus Stop*, as the road-weary nightclub singer Cherie, was another milestone in her acting career, surprising reviewers and even Logan himself, who declared she was a "comic genius." Even the famous Sir Laurence Olivier, who was patronizing to her when she co-starred with him in *The Prince and the Showgirl* (1957), would later admit that she stole the picture.

But along with professional success came an increasingly turbulent and unhappy personal life. There were men she fell for, lots of them, both very famous and not famous at all. Some, though by no means all, of the A-list names with which she was associated were: Frank Sinatra, Marlon Brando, Montgomery Clift, and Yves Montand. There were marriages to two celebrated figures outside the sphere of acting, both of whom she loved and admired but could not stay with. She married the legendary baseball player Joe DiMaggio in January 1954 and separated only nine months later, putting the failure of the marriage down to his resentment of her exhibitionist behavior and her fame. America's most respected playwright, Arthur Miller, who abandoned his wife and children to be with her, had a much stronger influence on her, but their 1956 marriage ended despairingly in 1961.

By then, her behavior had grown increasingly erratic and unpredictable. She attempted suicide more than once, was hospitalized for nervous disorders, abused prescription drugs and alcohol, and was notoriously, maddeningly late in showing up on the set and pretty much anywhere else in her life. It was as if all the success didn't really touch the core of her, the lonely, insecure girl who was never as central as she wanted to be in the minds and hearts of those she loved most.

In 1960 she made the less-than-stellar *Let's Make Love* and *The Misfits*, a film written by Arthur Miller especially for her, co-starring Clark Gable and Montgomery Clift. She disliked her part, in which she felt Miller was exposing her, through the character of Roslyn, as a vulnerable, unstable woman with a past she needed to hide. Her career ended in 1962 with the unfinished—and aptly named—*Something's Got to Give*, from which she was fired.

In 1961 actor Peter Lawford had introduced her to the Kennedys. JFK, now known to be an inveterate, even compulsive womanizer, began an affair with her but soon asked his brother Bobby to try to take her off his hands. It didn't work. In the end, nothing really did—not the men, not the movies, not the adulation of millions. She overdosed on sleeping pills and was found dead in her bed on the morning of August 5, 1962, at the age of 36, victim of either an intentional suicide or a tragic accident, brought on by the self-destructive impulses she had been battling for years.

But although Marilyn Monroe died, her legend and her image did not. If anything, death only burnished her glow, turning her into a latter-day martyr of sorts, an offering to the gods who seem to demand the young, the beautiful, the most tender and vulnerable as their due. She continues as a presence, not only in our hearts but in her best films, where she is reborn—gorgeous, giggly, impulsive, kind-hearted, infectiously happy. We continue to love her, and in that love her fragile spirit lives on.

NOW LET'S START TALKING ...

Over the following pages, Marilyn Monroe engages in an imaginary conversation covering fifteen themes, responding freely to searching questions.

The questions are in blue italic type;
Marilyn's answers are in pink type.

LITTLE GIRL LOST

The girl who became Marilyn Monroe had no family background in the conventional sense. Her father never held her in his arms, and she never found out who he was. Her mother suffered from serious mental illness and soon was unfit to care for her. As a result, she had no experience of what it was like to live with a mother and father, and this lack shaped her emotional life. What were her complex feelings about her parents? Did she wonder about her father, long for a closer relationship with her mother, imagine scenarios in which they might all be together?

Do you have many memories of your mother?

Not too many but a few things stand out. She was pretty. She had dark hair, creamy skin, and very fine, crisp features. And she spoke with a slight Scottish brogue. It had a lilting, musical sound. I liked hearing her say my name, and listening to her when she talked to her girlfriends on the telephone.

How much did you see of her when you were little?

She used to come visit me at one or other of the foster homes where I lived. I knew her only as a pretty lady who didn't smile much. When they told me to call her "Mama," I was surprised. She wasn't a person who had paid much attention to me. She didn't hug me or kiss me or even seem particularly interested in me. So calling her "Mama" seemed strange. Still, I did it anyway. I didn't know much about her then, but later, of course, I learned. And when I did, my heart hurt for both of us. I was very young when she was sent to a mental hospital. It was a terrible thing, you know? Losing my mother like that.

Did you ever live with her again, and if so, what was it like?

In the mid-1940s, when I was about 19, my mother decided she wanted to try living outside an institution. So she moved in with me. I was married to Jim at the time, but he was away, and so my mother and I shared an apartment. We even slept in the same bed. It was very touching how she wanted to help me—she did the cleaning, answered the phone, and took messages from the modeling agencies and studio casting agents who called me.

But at the same time, I confess that having her there became a burden. She expected me to support her. And sometimes she would go on these wild shopping sprees, and I'd have to pay for all the clothes she bought. Her mood swings were frightening, too. Eventually, I moved out, to the Studio Club, which was a rooming house for starlets.

Was she able to function on her own, without you?

Not really. She hardly ever went out after that. She got obsessed with religion, and the only person she saw much was Aunt Ana. After about seven months she went back to the hospital for good. I was sorry, but I won't deny that I was relieved, too. I felt I could concentrate on my own life again. She hadn't been much of a mother to me when I was little. I just wasn't ready to become a mother to *her* at that point.

Do you think that on some level she blamed you for what happened to her?

She probably did. My mother never wanted me. She was ashamed of getting pregnant, ashamed there was no husband around. So in some way she must have felt disgraced by having me. A divorced woman has enough problems getting a man, I guess, but one with an illegitimate baby. I wish ... I still wish she had wanted me.

Do you think your mother would have been proud of your success?

Yes, actually, I do, in spite of everything. She would have loved that I had made something of myself. Once, during the time she was out of the hospital and living with me, she got all dressed up in a white dress, white shoes, and a showy hat and paid a visit to Emmeline Snively, who ran the modeling agency she believed had saved me. "I only came so I could thank you personally for what you've been doing for Norma Jeane," she told her. "You've given her a whole new life."

What about your father? Were you told anything about him?

I was always told that my father had died in some kind of an accident. People used to say he was handsome—tall and slim. He had a mustache. But maybe that was just another lie—there were so many after all. Do you know, for a while I thought my father was Abraham Lincoln! He was my ideal. If I'd found my real father, I would have loved him with all my heart.

*You liked to call your husbands "Daddy." Do you think
Joe DiMaggio and Arthur Miller became father figures
for you?*

In the sense that they were both protective toward
me, yes, I guess they might have been. I liked it when
they took my side. But I don't mean I needed them to
tell me what to do. By the time I married them, I was
an adult with an established career.

*As an adult, you were often "mothered" by older women.
Do you see this as an outgrowth of your childhood
experiences?*

Yes, that was a pattern in my life. I remember "Aunt"
Grace and "Aunt" Ana—I loved them both so much,
and wanted nothing more than to please them. I guess
they felt I needed mothering, which I certainly did.

When I came to New York to work with Lee Strasberg, his wife Paula took me in and mothered me, too. So did my drama coach Natasha Lytess, back when I started getting film parts. I always felt in need of a mother, and older women just seemed to know that. They didn't mind mothering me. In fact, I think they actually liked it. I know I did.

Do you feel that your lack of a strong, cohesive family influenced the choices you made later in your life?

Absolutely. I grew up on a kind of emotional fault line—there was never any solid ground under my feet. So I didn't know what stability felt like, and even though it was something I longed for, I didn't have a clue about how to find it.

MODEL BEHAVIOR

It is now well known that Marilyn got her start
not as an actress, but as a photographer's model.
What is less widely known is how she felt about
her modeling work, or how she saw it in the
context of her later life. Modeling turned out to
be a pivotal experience for her, and brought
her both satisfaction and success. She put hard
work into learning the business and eventually
developed an extraordinary ability to look relaxed
and natural for the still camera—a talent that
impressed many photographers in her publicity
work for films.

When did you start thinking of becoming a model?

It was when some army photographers came by
the parachute factory where I worked and asked
if they could take my picture. I was surprised,
but I went along with it. It was more fun than
inspecting parachutes, I can tell you that. I liked the
photographers taking an interest in me. They were
always very nice, gave me lots of compliments and
encouragement. I wasn't used to that but I remember
thinking I could get used to it pretty quickly.

What was the initial appeal modeling had for you?
Was it just the attention?

No, it wasn't just that. As a model, I made five
dollars an hour. So in one day of modeling, I could
make what it took me a week to make at the plant.

Are you saying it was mostly about the money?

Well, the money was important, of course. After all,
I'd never had much of it. But then I found that I loved
to pose. I was amazed at how the pictures made me
look better than in real life. In the pictures, I felt
like I was someone else—someone different, special,
better. In the pictures, I looked like I was loved.

Later on, how successful were you as a model?

Well, I was on five magazine covers—although some
of them were different issues of the same magazine.
They just posed me differently—outside, inside.
Mostly, though, I was just sitting there, looking out
over the ocean. And they showed lots of legs and
backside, you know? All those cheesecake shots.
But that's what people wanted, so that's what I did.

It's a way to make people happy and catch their attention, too. You can prove yourself later on.

You certainly caught the eye in the famous Life *magazine feature where you impersonated other great actresses. Was that in 1958?*

Yes, Richard Avedon took those pictures. I posed for him as Lillian Russell, Theda Bara, Clara Bow, Jean Harlow, and Marlene Dietrich. People were surprised that I managed to portray them so convincingly. But I could make my face do anything, same as you can take a white board and build from that and make a painting.

What about your pin-up nude modeling session for the calendar in 1949? Can you talk a bit about that experience?

There was this photographer, Tom Kelly, who'd been after me for ages to pose nude. I'd always said no, because I just hadn't wanted to do that. But the price for nude modeling was 50 dollars an hour, and at that point I was behind on my rent at the Hollywood Studio Club and I really, really needed the money. So I called Tom and asked, "How soon can we do it?," and he said tomorrow. I asked Tom not to have anyone else there but his wife, Natalie. She was a doll. They were both incredibly sweet to me, and made me feel very relaxed and natural. Tom took only two poses—one with me sitting up, and the other with me lying down. I liked the one of me lying down the best. And so did Tom—that's the one he sold to the calendar company. It was actually a very lovely and even tasteful photograph. It suggested more than it revealed.

What was the reaction of the studio when they found out you'd done this?

Total frenzy. They were so worried, they called me on the set where I was working to find out if it was true, if I'd really done it. When I said that yes, I had, the poor guy who asked me nearly had a stroke. But in the end, the publicity I got from that whole incident helped me a lot. It gave me a little extra allure, you know? A little something special that made me stand out in the crowd. Now I was the girl who had Done That. Everyone knew about me, and for an aspiring actress that was a very, very good thing. Back then, some people thought it was scandalous, of course, especially when the picture became the centerfold in the launch of *Playboy*. But I think a lot of others were impressed that I was frank about having done it.

Do you think starting out as a model harmed your chances of being taken seriously as an actress? Did those nude photos contribute to your being typecast as a sex goddess?

Oh God, yes. But I didn't have much choice back then. In my business, you needed every little edge you could get, so I had to use what I had. Anyway, I wasn't going to be ashamed of the nudity. I wanted a man to come home from a hard day's work, look at this picture, and feel inspired to say, "Wow!"

FLEDGLING ACTRESS

She had the kind of looks that made us want
never to stop looking. The creamy skin, the
incandescent smile, the open yet dreamy gaze.
Hers was a face on which the camera loved to
linger. Her milky, abundant flesh practically
spilled out of the silver screen and into our laps.
But Marilyn wanted to be valued for more than
her body. When she left Hollywood to study
with Lee Strasberg at The Actors Studio in New
York, Marilyn struggled to deepen her craft.
She yearned to play serious stage parts. But her
aspirations were often mocked or twisted into
lewd jest.

Did you always want to be an actress?

Yes, I did. But I didn't admit it to myself. I felt so unworthy—ignorant and untrained. I didn't know a single thing about acting. And I would have been too ashamed to tell anyone about my dreams.

Can you talk about your goals as an actress, as distinct from your success as a Hollywood film personality?

I know that it was my looks that gave me my start— everyone loves a pretty girl, and I was very, very pretty. But while that would have been enough—no, more than enough—for some people, it wasn't enough for me. I wanted more for myself. *From* myself. I believed I had it in me. I really did. I was already a big success when I went to New York to study with Lee Strasberg, and I didn't have to go—

no one made me, or even encouraged me. But I wanted to, even though going scared the pants off me. The work was hard, and the self-exposure Lee demanded was even harder.

I knew I wasn't a fine actress. In fact I often felt third-rate, like I was wearing cheap clothes on the inside. But my God how I wanted to learn, to change, to improve! Why wouldn't anyone believe that? When I said I was trying to develop, to sharpen my skills, I was mocked, laughed at. I liked to laugh, you know? But I didn't like being turned into a walking joke.

What would you say was your greatest strength as an actress?

Arthur Miller thought my ability to play comedy had a lot to do with my curiosity about other people— how closely I used to watch them. When you're an observer, you notice things, little details of gesture and voice that someone who's more of a participant would miss. I was always watching, listening, trying to figure things out. That's because I felt like an outsider—an outsider who desperately wanted to find her way in. Later on, when my career took off, people used to tell me I made them feel happy when they were watching me. I guess that's a talent, too.

Do you feel actors in general—and you in particular— have to be natural extroverts?

Not at all. Most actors have to overcome shyness, and I was about the most self-conscious actress who ever stepped in front of a camera. It was a real struggle for me to begin a new role. Every time I got up to act, I felt like I was in some deep, dark cave and had to claw my way out. There was always a certain amount of pain in the experience. I found it terribly hard to act parts that didn't seem real to me, to my own character.

The process you describe does sound painful. Did you ever find pleasure in acting?

Yes, I did find pleasure in my work. Acting was something golden and beautiful. It wasn't an art. It was like a game you played that enabled you to step out of the dull world you knew into worlds so bright it made your heart leap just to think of them. So it was that feeling of escape and expansion that made the hard parts all worthwhile.

SEX AND THE SINGLE STARLET

Sex appeal—Monroe had it all right. In spades. At times, the throb and heat created by her visual presence had to be turned into a dirty joke to diffuse its explosive charge. So many of her leading men were not her equals. Even when she was paired with the undeniably virile Clark Gable in *The Misfits*, he was old enough—quite literally—to have been her father. But the real story of Monroe's sexuality was far more complex than her sex-kitten screen persona ever permitted anyone to see.

You were called a sex goddess by Hollywood, the press,
and your fans. Sexual appeal was your passport and
your currency for so many years. But what are your real
feelings about sex? How was your sexuality used—or
misused—in your life?

Oh, don't get me started on sex. I could write a book
on the subject, I really could. It all started young for
me. When I was eight, a boarder who lived with one
of my foster families touched me in a way I didn't
like—it made me feel dirty. I told on him, but no one
believed me. Not only that, but also I got in trouble
for telling, so I learned not to tell anymore. As I got
older, boys started to notice me. And I liked their
attention, I really did. I was married by the time I
was 16. I think they thought it would calm me down
somehow. Contain and corral all that sexual energy
that had only just started to bubble up in me.

You can't ask me to reduce what I think about sex to just a single attitude or feeling. Sex is such a huge, complex part of life. It means different things at different moments. The trouble is, being a sex symbol means being a "thing." And I didn't especially want to be a thing. All the same, there are worse things to symbolize than sex.

We know how sexy the world thought you were. But did you consider yourself to be a sexy woman?

Not particularly. When I was young, I didn't dream about sex, or long for it. That's because I felt so bad about myself then—it's hard to feel sexy when you feel worthless.

It's been said that you had sex for money. Is there any truth in that?

When I was quite young and still married to Jim
Dougherty, while he was away with the Merchant
Marine, a man in a bar said he would give me fifteen
dollars if I went to a hotel with him. I was shocked.
But fifteen dollars was so much money! Since I was
kind of drunk at the time, I agreed. Besides, he
was wearing a suit, so I didn't think he would hurt
me—can you imagine anyone being so naïve? I went
with him and he asked me to take off my clothes.
I thought it was a pretty good deal for fifteen dollars.
I didn't actually have sex with him. But later on,
I still felt kind of crummy about it. I never did
anything like that again, even when I was hard up.

What did you find sexy in a man?

The sexiest men are the ones who can make a
woman feel sexy. Not the ones who think of sex

as a competitive sport. A good lover can make you melt just by the way he touches your hair or smiles into your eyes.

Did you enjoy sex or was it mostly a way of seeking affection or love, or trying to assuage your loneliness?

When I was young, I did use sex as a way to seek affection, but I don't think that's so unusual. Offering your body as a way to fill up your heart is a kind of classic part of the female psyche. There was also a period when I just slept around too much, sometimes to help my career, sometimes because I was flattered when men took an interest in me. They were always so full of self-confidence, and I had none at all then. I always liked the guys, and they made me feel better. But you don't get self-confidence that way. You have to get it by earning respect.

As I got a little older and a little more sure
of myself, I did have some extraordinary sexual
experiences. Love was always a part of them, though.
If there are going to be fireworks, you need love to
ignite them.

ON THE SILVER SCREEN

Marilyn is remembered more for who she was than for the roles she played in her films. Many of her admirers felt that the parts she was given were not equal to her talents, and she herself had mixed feelings about them. Yet most of her films were very successful, and she quickly became famous. She knew that fame is fleeting, yet the desire for it propelled her and egged her on. She needed fame the way she needed air, even if her relationship to her own success was often contradictory and she remained insecure about her abilities as an actress.

Many of your films were musicals. Did you enjoy the singing and dancing you were required to do?

Dancing on set was not the easiest thing for me. Off it, I loved dancing with some guy I was crazy for, but those big musical numbers were a strain. Singing was another story, though. Even though I didn't have much training, I loved to sing—it made me feel both exhilarated and calm at the same time. Numbers like "Diamonds Are a Girl's Best Friend" were a lot of fun to record—they were so upbeat and peppy. And I loved Irving Berlin's songs in *There's No Business Like Show Business*. He was a musical genius. "Heat Wave," "Lazy," "You'd Be Surprised"… all of them immortal, wonderful show tunes. It was truly an honor to get to sing them.

What about theater? Did you ever want to do that?

I so badly wanted to act on stage, especially after I'd been in New York and worked with Lee. But I didn't want to be confined to just comedies or other light stuff the way I had been on screen. I wanted to break out of that mold and do serious drama.

Did you ever consider directing films?

The studio joke was that I wanted to direct pictures and I couldn't direct traffic. But it might have been fun to direct a film. I'd have made sure the women got to play real roles, though. I'd have been respectful of all the actors, women and men alike.

Some critics feel that Some Like It Hot *was your best film. Do you agree?*

I couldn't see it at the time. I thought I'd be stuck

playing dumb blondes forever. And it was a difficult time for me, shooting that movie. Later on, though, I came to appreciate the comic genius of the film. It has great dialogue and great pacing. I played a not very bright band singer, but in the end I came to see that my character was more than just dumb. She was trusting, she was innocent, and in the end she was worthy of winning the heart of the guy she loved.

Which of your films was your least favorite and why?

I'd have to say the script of *Let's Make Love* was pretty ridiculous, but then you might say all of my films with Fox when I played one-dimensional, stupid women were ridiculous. There were a lot of other films I didn't enjoy shooting, like *Bus Stop* and *The Prince and the Showgirl*, where I felt directors were trying to push me around instead of letting me do it my way. People who said I was difficult on the set in my later films never took into account how angry those directors made me feel.

The success of Gentlemen Prefer Blondes *really put you into a whole different category, didn't it? Would you say that was a pivotal film in your career?*

Yes, I became a star, but the studio wasn't treating me like one. I was on $500 a week and my co-star, Jane Russell, was getting $200,000 for the picture. Even though I was a sensation, I still didn't have a dressing room of my own. I got down to the level of pointing out that the movie was *Gentlemen Prefer Blondes* and I *was* the blonde. I mean, why did I even have to say that?

To what director or studio would you ascribe your fame?

My fame didn't come from a director or studio. It was the public who chose to make me famous, because they knew, deep down, I was one of them. I never felt superior or above them. I'd grown up poor and unloved. I didn't have much of an education. I wasn't some princess, born with a silver spoon in my mouth. Instead, I shared their dreams, and they felt like my success held some promise for them.

What was your reaction when you learned about your first major movie deal?

When *Gentlemen Prefer Blondes* came out, I was happy—incredibly happy. I remember driving back and forth in front of the theater just to see my name up there on the marquee. I even wished "Marilyn Monroe" had been "Norma Jeane" so that all the kids who'd ignored me at school and in the orphanage would know it was me. I wanted to be seen, you know? That's what fame meant for me—being seen and acknowledged, maybe for the first time.

Did you mind all the gossip that was written and said about you?

Gossip is just words, and anyone can say anything. I suppose I was grateful for the attention, even if sometimes the things that were said were lies, and cruel besides. When you're famous, you can read someone else's version of who you are, but in the end, none of that matters. You have to know the truth about yourself, and when you do, no one can take it from you.

Were the people you had known supportive of you when you became famous? How did they react to your success?

So many people I'd known were not kind, not supportive, and not happy. They were envious— envy coated their faces like a layer of green paint. But I learned to disregard it. After all, I was famous and they were envious, right? So who was in the better position?

Did your fame bring you happiness?

Yes, I was happy at first, but it wasn't the sort of feeling that lasted. And there were times when being famous didn't seem quite real to me. I felt as though it was all happening to someone right next to me. It was close, I could feel it, I could hear it, but it wasn't really me who was experiencing it.

DOLLARS AND DIAMONDS

When Marilyn died in 1962, she didn't leave a fortune—no Beverly Hills mansion, imported cars, yachts, or racehorses. She had a lot of clothes, but little jewelry of consequence at the time. Lots of books, but no priceless works of art. Her most valuable piece of furniture was the lacquered white, baby grand piano that once belonged to her mother. The relative modesty of her estate suggests that she simply was not all that interested in money. Perhaps she knew happiness wasn't something she could buy.

What was your relationship to money? Was it a powerful motivating force in your life?

When I was young I didn't want to be rich. I just wanted people to think I was wonderful. Starting out in the movie business, I would be invited to parties, chiefly as decoration—I believe you call it "arm candy" these days. I watched men betting thousands of dollars in casual card games and it disgusted me. I grew up poor, and to me, such behavior was beyond extravagant—it was wasteful, it was obscene. I knew how ordinary people had to skimp and work all hours just to get through the week.

Did your attitude to money make you an oddity in Hollywood?

Did it ever! Hollywood was based on money. But

I never let money influence my heart, and I never married for it either. I easily could have. Johnny Hyde, the agent, was a very rich man who wanted me. And I liked Johnny, I really did. Like and love were not the same, though. I wasn't going to let money blur the distinction.

It's been said that you donated a lot of money to children's causes, and to orphanages. Is that true?

Yes, I did give a lot of money to institutions or groups who worked with children. I think the reasons are pretty obvious. My own experience as an orphan left such deep scars—I wanted to keep other children from having those same scars. I know money can't buy a family, or love. But money can buy a kid nice shoes, a decent dress. It can help someone feel less worthless, less like a beggar.

What were your main indulgences? Clothes? Jewelry?

I loved clothes and did buy a lot of them once I was earning enough to do that. But I was never a slave to fashion. I thought clothes should work for me, not the other way around.

What was the most beautiful dress you ever owned?

It has to be the one I wore when I sang "Happy Birthday" to John F. Kennedy. What a dress that was! It was made of flesh-colored gauze and was encrusted with graduated rhinestones in a rosette motif. The material was virtually sculpted onto my naked body. It cost $12,000. Can you imagine? They said the dress was too revealing. But who cares if it shocked some people? I had the guts to wear it, and it made me feel special, rare, uniquely prized.

Who were some of your favorite designers?

I loved Emilio Pucci—I had lots of his dresses and tops, in both solids and his signature prints. I owned a Pucci handbag, along with a lot of other Pucci accessories. Those clothes had such a sense of whimsy to them—I always felt playful and lighthearted when I wore Pucci. Kind of like a kid. Norman Norel made me a stunning green sequined evening gown that I wore at the Golden Globe awards in 1962. That dress was like a starburst—you just couldn't not look at it, or the girl who was wearing it. I needed to feel ready to put on a dress like that, ready to wield the power it gave me. I also loved the designers Lanvin and Galanos. But those clothes were different—they were more formal, and conservative. In some ways, they were like donning a suit of armor. I felt remote and untouchable when

I wore their clothes. Sometimes, a dress by Lanvin was just the defense I needed against the world.

What kinds of shoes did you like?

Stiletto-heeled pumps by Salvatore Ferragamo. I used to order them in all different materials and colors: scarlet satin with matching rhinestones, black satin with a cluster of rhinestones at the toe. They changed not only the way I walked, but the way I used my whole body. Spike heels make you teeter a bit, you always look unsteady, as if the least little tip could push you right over, onto your back. Guys liked that look.

Did you buy a lot of jewelry?

Yes, but even though I was famous for the song, "Diamonds Are a Girl's Best Friend," most of what

I bought and wore was fake. Kind of funny when you think about it, isn't it? But the real stuff didn't matter much to me, not when the fake looked so good. I mean, I could tell the difference between champagne and beer—but not between the most expensive pearls from the South Seas and a phony strand, so why spend all that money on the real thing?

CREATURE COMFORTS

Marilyn had an abiding love for all animals.
As an adult, she took her pets—dogs, even
parakeets—with her when she went on location
or traveled. And as a child and young woman,
she was utterly devoted to the animals that
crossed her path, even when she had little or
no ability to help them. Her love for them, and
her anguish when they suffered, came across
powerfully in *The Misfits*, in which Arthur
Miller's script was built around the character
she played—a woman shocked when she watched
her cowboy friends roping wild horses to be
turned into dog meat.

Would you describe yourself as a lover of animals?

Yes, I've always felt a keen connection to almost all animals, a kind of deep sympathy or communion. I can't stand to see them confined or mistreated. Once, I saw two boys with pigeons they had caught and were planning to sell—I paid them to set all the pigeons free. My husband Jim used to hunt. He would sometimes ask me to clean or cook what he'd caught, which I couldn't bear. One time, he'd shot a deer that regained consciousness in the car on the way home. I was horrified when I saw it struggling, and I begged him to set it free. He didn't, though—he strangled it to put it out of its misery. I wouldn't talk to him for days … Another time, I saw this cow that one of our neighbors had tied up and left standing in the rain. There it was, all alone and soaked, not making one sound of protest. It just tore me up. I wanted to bring it into our apartment rather than leave it out there, though of course Jim thought I was crazy and wouldn't let me.

Did you have any pets?

When I was a little girl, I had a small dog named Tippy. He had brown eyes that always followed me, watched me everywhere I went. I never experienced that kind of devotion before, and it completely won me over. He went with me to school, and waited in the yard until I was dismissed, and then went home with me again. Then one night he disappeared. I think a neighbor shot him. But I couldn't prove it. I still remember how devastated I was. And the worst part was that the feeling was so familiar, as if I'd lived it all before. Later on, I had a white Maltese named "Maf." I always traveled with a pet—a dog, or a parakeet. Do you like parakeets? I love them for their bright, cheerful disposition, those little black eyes looking at you, the crazy colors of their feathers. Parakeets are like sunshine on a perch.

Can you say what it was that you liked about animals?

Animals are loyal, constant, and completely without artifice. A dog doesn't love you because you're famous or beautiful—a dog loves you just because you are you. And they're very responsive to human moods. A dog will lick your tears away, or just sit by your side when you feel lonely and blue. And when you're happy, your dog's happy too. Your happiness is enough for him.

LEGENDARY LOVES

Marilyn's love life has become the stuff of legend. The roster of powerful, take-charge, alpha men with whom she was linked was formidable, and included both President John F. Kennedy and his younger brother, Senator Robert Kennedy. But despite her many, much-publicized romances, Marilyn was unable to forge a bond that lasted. She married three times, and not one of those marriages brought her the peace and satisfaction she craved. Yet she seemed perpetually optimistic on the subject, and believed that one day she would find the right partner in love and in life.

What was it about powerful men that attracted you?

The way they took charge of their lives was thrilling to me. I wanted that power for myself. It was almost as if I could get it by sleeping with them, you know? When I was very young, I had this thing with Joe Schenk. He was the head of the Fox studio, and a very important man. I used to go over to his house—it was a mansion, with the finest drapes, carpets, and furniture. And he served delicious food. He's the one who taught me about champagne. Mr. Schenk loved my breasts. After dinner, he'd ask me to take off my clothes and snuggle up next to him. He'd tell me stories about all the stars he'd known, like John Barrymore, Charlie Chaplin, and Valentino, and play with my breasts while he talked. But that was pretty much all we did. He was kind of old by then. Sometimes, he'd ask me to kiss him down there. I did it, too. It seemed to go on for hours, but nothing ever happened. Usually, he fell asleep, but if he stayed awake, he'd pat my head, like I was a little dog.

Later, I had flings with both Marlon Brando and Yves Montand. You know, they talk about animal magnetism—I think Marlon had it without even doing anything. That magnificent head and torso, and the way he moved like a dancer. His whole body kind of rippled when he walked ... Yves was another very sexy man. He always reminded me of Joe DiMaggio. And I adored his French accent. I loved him but he told me he'd never leave Simone [Signoret]. Never. I think I fell for him even harder when Simone won the Best Actress Oscar. Although she and I were friends, that made me so jealous that I felt like saying, "You've got the Oscar, but I've got Yves." Now that was kind of childish of me, I know. But in matters of the heart, we can all be childish, don't you think?

Do you think it was wrong to sleep with married men?

Not really. If a man strays, it's because he's unhappy with his wife. Happy men don't stray. Or else he's a womanizer, and a womanizer will always cheat, because that's his nature. If he weren't cheating with me, it would be with someone else.

What about JFK? Did it give you a huge charge to sleep with a president?

Of course! He was such a vital, brilliant, charismatic guy. So young, too. You never thought of a president being so young. One time, we were seated together at a big, fancy dinner. He kept putting his hand on my thigh under the table. But he didn't let it stay there—it kept creeping up, higher and higher. Then he realized I wasn't wearing any underwear—I hardly ever did, you know. He pulled his hand away and his face turned pink. I'll bet he never put his hand up Jackie's dress. She was too stiff, too prim. I think he admired her, but I don't think he loved her.

Weren't you involved with Bobby Kennedy as well?

No. That rumor was not true. I liked him, but not physically. He didn't have the aura that his brother did, but I loved his mind. On the phone he always seemed like a soul-mate. We even joked about marrying each other. Of course, that never would have worked out. Can you picture it—me, married to a high-profile celebrity like that? The press would have crucified me. Oh, I forgot—they did that anyway.

Looking back, who would you say was the great love of your life?

There wasn't a single great love. I've had several. Joe DiMaggio was one. I almost called off my first meeting with Joe. I was so tired the night of our first date, and wanted to get out of it. But I went anyway. I imagined a very different kind of guy—slick, black hair, flashy clothes, and a smooth line of New York patter. But instead, there was this choirboy. No line at all. No jokes either. He was shy and serious but also very warm, very friendly. During dinner, I saw that he wasn't eating, he was just looking at me. And suddenly, I wasn't tired any more. After that, we were together all the time. I thought he had the power and grace of a Michelangelo sculpture. And he had a big, big heart. I loved that about him.

Can you talk a bit about your other two marriages?
How would you characterize the marriage to your first
husband, Jim Dougherty?

Jim was a sweet boy, but he was just a boy, in the same way that I was just a girl. And boys and girls really shouldn't get married. They just aren't ready. You could call our marriage a sort of friendship with sexual privileges. A lot of marriages are no more than that, and a lot of men make better lovers when they're betraying their wives.

When you married the playwright Arthur Miller, people called you, "The Beauty and the Brain." What was your relationship really like?

When I first met him, I was smitten. I felt like I'd been thirsty for years, and he was the cool, sweet water I'd been craving. It was the first time I really felt like I was in love. Arthur was serious—but playful, too. We laughed and joked all the time. I was crazy for him. He promised to make my life different.

Different and better. I loved his mind and he loved mine. We used to talk, and I mean really talk, for hours. I felt like I could tell him anything and everything. And he listened. Arthur was not about surfaces, he was about depth. He cared. He saw what Hollywood was doing to me. He wouldn't let it happen. He promised.

Which men hurt you most?

It's always the ones you love the most that can hurt you the most. Like Joe. He wanted a very traditional sort of wife—one who'd cook his favorite dishes, like lasagna or spaghetti and meatballs, and spend hours waxing the kitchen floor and starching his shirts. And even though he thought I was beautiful and sexy, he didn't want anyone else to see me that way. He thought I should dress in these really modest clothes, like high-necked blouses with Peter Pan collars. Can you imagine me in drab getup like that? Joe was jealous of my success. When I did that street scene for *The Seven Year Itch* where my skirt blew up and all those people were watching, he was furious. Furious! We had a huge fight that night and, though I hate to say this about him, he hit me. And it wasn't the first time either. Or the last. That man definitely had a temper. The end came pretty quickly after that. But I wish it had worked out with him. I used to ask myself, what's the point of being a sex star if it drives your man away? Even after we broke up, Joe was my best friend in the world, especially when I was sick or in trouble. He thought no one could love me except him, and there was a time after *The Misfits* when we thought about remarrying.

In the end, Arthur Miller hurt me, too. He thought I wanted too much, that I was too needy. I found some notes he'd written about me, as if I were just "material" for his writing. He'd written that at first he believed I was some kind of angel, but that he no longer felt that way. And that although his first wife had disappointed him, it was nothing compared to what I'd done to him. Those were terrible, terrible things to read. The last straw was when he wrote *The Misfits* as a vehicle for me. I hated the film, and I hated the part he wrote for me, too. He depicted the character I was playing as crazy. To stop the men in the film roping down horses to be killed, I had to throw a screaming, crazy fit. I mean, I had to go completely nuts. I thought, why is he doing this to me? He could have written it any number of ways to show me as humane and able to explain why it was wrong to hunt those horses down. Yet he came up with a crazed woman. If he really thought I was that, then I wasn't for him and he wasn't for me.

Do you think there may have been some truth in what
Arthur Miller was saying—that you were too needy?
Do you think your neediness was, in part, the reason
your marriages broke up?

I've asked myself that question many, many times.
There are moments when I thought that yes, it was
something deficient in me that caused the break-
ups, that I needed so much, more than anyone could
reasonably be expected to give. But there were other
times when I thought differently. I mean, isn't that
what love's all about? Giving yourself over to another
person's needs? That's what I was willing to do, that's
what I tried to do. Why wasn't anyone willing to do it
for *me*? I never could answer that question.

Which relationships would you like to have given
another try?

A man I really regretted losing was Frank Sinatra. He wouldn't have expected me to be a housewife—we both could have had our careers. It would have been perfect. But I couldn't tie him down, not Frankie. He was one that got away, if you know what I mean. I had a few of those in my life …

Do you have any advice about marriage that you would like to share?

Yes. I think people should marry for love, and only love, not for sexual attraction or for money. By love I mean what I said before—a feeling or an impulse that's primarily selfless, not selfish. Get to know the person you're going to marry. Be sure you can make it through the tough times, because God knows, you're going to have those, no matter who you are. And one last thing: marriage should be fun—not just hard work and sacrifice, but plain, old-fashioned fun, with a real delight in one another's company. That's the kind of thing that lasts.

HOLLYWOOD PEOPLE

As a screen personality, Marilyn was associated
with many of the best actors and directors of her
day. At the height of her fame, she was firmly
ensconced on the A-list, and even heavyweights
like Sir Laurence Olivier wanted a piece of
the monetary action she generated. Some of
these luminaries she found were pure pleasure
to work with; others, pure hell. But they still
wanted to work with her, and she left a lasting
impression on them. Eventually, she also showed
her studio that she was not a woman to be taken
lightly. She could fight for her rights and win.

You had some rough times when you started out in Hollywood. How did you change that around?

At first I was a stupid kid who thought I could make it just by working the party circuit like all the other starlets—being a good-time girl, and hoping someone would pick me out as special. I lived to regret that, and it didn't bring me the parts I wanted anyway. I saw more than I wanted to of the nasty end of the business, and there's no doubt that it changed me, made me tougher and more determined. I always got on well with guys in the press—reporters and photographers—and they taught me a lot about how to publicize myself. I also got to know who had real power in the studio, and set out to get myself noticed by the people who were right at the top, like Spyros Skouras—the head of Twentieth Century Fox.

Who helped you most in getting beyond bit parts?

More than anyone, my first agent, Johnny Hyde. He not only loved me but believed I could become a star. He persuaded John Huston to let me read for *The Asphalt Jungle*, and that was the first time anyone took me seriously as an actress. Then my acting coach, Natasha Lytess, who was with me from 1948 when I got my six-month contract with Columbia. She gave me the education I'd never had, as well as coaching me. Another friend, and lover, who had real influence in Hollywood at that time was Elia Kazan, who supported me when my career hit a rocky patch.

Which were your favorite on-set relationships?

I was a sucker for John Huston. I remember my audition for him … I was so nervous. I thought that

if I could take my shoes off, I'd feel more relaxed.
So he told me to go ahead and take them off. In the
scene, I was supposed to be lying on the couch, only
there was no couch, so I asked if I could lie down on
the floor. Again the answer was yes. Then I wanted
to do the scene one more time, because I thought I
hadn't done my best. He said it wasn't necessary, but
in the end he let me do that, too. He was incredibly
patient. And then, after all that, he told me he had
decided to give me the part the first time around.

Joshua Logan was another very patient director.
Boy, did we have some rows making *Bus Stop*, but
at the end he told me that I was one of the most
unappreciated actresses in the world, and that I was
worth all the trouble.

As for actors, I loved working with Tommy
Noonan in *Gentlemen Prefer Blondes*. He was a total
honey, and I adored him. One of my true idols,

though, was Clark Gable. You asked me before about father figures, and he really was one for me. According to Freud, that's a natural and healthy kind of association to have. Clark never got angry with me once, for blowing a line, or being late, or anything. He never raised his voice, lost his temper. He was a gentleman, the best. I used to get so nervous around him. I didn't want to disappoint him or make him angry, and somehow that just made things worse. The nicer he was, the more I screwed up. Kind of strange, wasn't it?

Montgomery Clift was with you and Gable in The Misfits. *Did you have a good relationship with him?*

I'd heard people sneering at him for being homosexual, people who weren't fit to open a door for him. What did they know about it? Labels—people love putting labels on each other. I took no notice of all that. In fact, I did my best to seduce him. It didn't work, but I sure tried. You know, in spite of the rumors I don't think anything happened between him and Elizabeth Taylor either. He was a mess … but I still loved him. So many women did. I guess we thought we could "cure" him, you know? Liz thought the same thing. Drop-dead gorgeous as Monty was, he never made me nervous the way Gable did. Monty and I were more alike in some way. I sensed the fragility in him, the damage. And so I was never afraid of him. We were good pals, Monty and I. Brother and sister even.

Which working relationships did you find difficult?

Tony Curtis was my leading man in *Some Like It Hot*, one of my most successful films. But he was a misery as a co-star. Because I kept arguing with Billy Wilder, Tony thought I was behaving like a dictator on the set. So he said that kissing me was like kissing Adolf Hitler. But I really don't think the trouble between us was all my fault—far from it. He had a very controlling, difficult, even manic personality. He wasn't flexible at all. If he thought kissing me was like kissing Hitler, then I could say that kissing him was like kissing Mussolini.

Then there was Larry—Sir Laurence Olivier—who was both my director and my co-star in *The Prince and the Showgirl*. Larry was such an extraordinary actor. I was in awe of his training, his talent, and his delivery. But he was very condescending to me and it made me feel terrible. Also, angry. After all, he wasn't above wanting to do a film with me because he thought my name would make it a huge success at the box office. So what did he have to act so superior about?

And I could spend a week just talking about Billy Wilder. Everyone on the set had to do it his way. But I can also acknowledge that Billy was a great director and had a wild streak that no one could match. I wish he could have come up with another vehicle for me, though—a screenplay where I wasn't just funny, but smart, too.

Who were the greatest directors of your generation?

Here is the wish list I made for the people at Fox: George Cukor, John Ford, Alfred Hitchcock, John Huston, Elia Kazan, David Lean, Joshua Logan, Joseph Mankiewicz, Vicente Minnelli, Carol Reed, Vittorio de Sica, George Stevens, Lee Strasberg, Billy Wilder, William Wyler, and Fred Zimmerman. Stellar directors, every last one of them. Some I got to work with, others I could only dream about.

You were a very gifted comedienne. What male comedians did you like?

I liked Jerry Lewis. He had all this vitality and energy. And he also had a very nice face—he only made all these funny faces because that's what people expected from him. I met Jerry once at a radio show. I liked Dean Martin, too. He was a friend of Jerry's. The two of them would start howling and falling all over the place when they saw me. It was a great gag we all had going.

How did other Hollywood actresses treat you when you became famous?

Some, like Jane Russell, were quite wonderful to me. Others, like Anna Magnani, were really bitchy. I was at an awards ceremony with Magnani, and afterwards

I heard her hiss "Putana"—whore—when I went to sit down. Pretty mean, huh?

What other actresses did you admire, and why?

I was a huge fan of Jean Harlow. I just thought she lit up the screen whenever she was on it. It was the eyes, I think—so expressive, and so alert. A couple of people said I reminded them of her—I was really flattered by that. I also loved the Hepburns— Katharine and Audrey—because they both were so cool and elegant, each in her own way. And Bette Davis was a great, great actress, one who could play anything and anyone. If someone said, "Bette, be a tree," she'd be the leafiest, greenest, most alive tree in the whole damn forest. There was nothing she couldn't do. God, I admired that woman. I wish I'd had the chance to work with Harlow and Davis—

I know I'd have learned a lot from each of them,
though what I learned would have been really,
really different.

THE LIFE OF THE MIND

The dumb blonde image was like glue—it stuck and wouldn't come off. But Marilyn possessed her own quirky kind of intelligence. The twittering, vacuous screen image hid what Arthur Miller called her "perceptive naïveté," and she could be witty. Her lack of formal education made her want to find out how things got to be the way they were. Books and the people who wrote them became a deep interest for her. She loved reading, tried her hand at writing, and was curious about some of the intellectual currents of the day, even if she couldn't funnel that interest directly into her screen work.

You've been close to quite a few intellectuals. Did you ever yourself have any aspirations in that direction?

Don't be silly, I never thought of myself as an intellectual or had any desire to be one. But I did have a lot of admiration for people who *were* intellectual. I really enjoyed talking to them, hearing their points of view, the way they looked at things. It gave me a sense of space, of freedom, inside. Like I was opening up a window, wide, and letting in all the fresh air. Once, an astrologer pointed out that I'd been born under Gemini, the same sign as Rosalind Russell, Judy Garland, and Mickey Rooney. I had an answer for that one: "Yes, and I was born under the same sign as Ralph Waldo Emerson, Queen Victoria, and Walt Whitman." Still, I always felt insecure about my ability to cope with people who knew much more than me. I never graduated from high school, and I considered myself dumb for such a long time.

Did intellectuals make you doubt yourself or feel you had no value?

Well, I had a lot of friends that I would consider "intellectual." Truman Capote was a close friend of mine. He was as funny as he was smart, so that's saying a lot. God, but we had some great times. And of course, Arthur—I ended up marrying him, as you know. Mostly, these super brainy, intellectual people nonetheless found something to admire in me. Vladimir Nabokov called me one of the great comedy actresses of our time and said I was simply superb. Can you imagine it? The man who wrote *Lolita*, one of the most important and brilliant books of the century, said that, about me. I was so proud when I heard it. One of the poets whose work I most liked, Carl Sandburg, didn't see me as the usual kind of movie idol. He thought there was something democratic about me, that I was someone who would pitch in and wash up the supper dishes without waiting to be asked. Now wasn't that a nice thing to have said? He didn't think I was a diva. He understood something about me, how I never saw any reason for pretense. I actually met Carl, and we spent the evening together. He was such fun to be with—a true blithe spirit. We danced, and you know what?—he was a terrific dancer, very old world, even courtly in his manner. It was a magical night.

Diana Trilling, the literati queen, said it was impossible to think of me as anything other than Cinderella. I wasn't so crazy about being called that. Who wants to be Cinderella, just waiting for the prince and his stupid glass slipper to rescue you?

I was never Cinderella. Everything that happened to me happened because I made it happen. My success was the result of my hard work, my determination, and my grit. I was my own fairy godmother, so don't let anyone say otherwise. I'll tell you a remark about me that I did like, though. The abstract painter Franz Kline said he thought that if you bit me, milk and honey would flow from the spot. It takes an artist to say a thing like that.

Were you a big reader? If so, what did you like to read?

I did love to read, though I never seemed to have the time to read all the books that I wanted to. Still, I had a personal library of more than 400 books. I seldom read a book straight through, though. I used to dip in and out of a book, like I was tasting it. Some of the books I admired were Jack Kerouac's

On the Road, D.H. Lawrence's *Sons and Lovers*, Ralph Ellison's *The Invisible Man*, and Scott Fitzgerald's *The Great Gatsby*. Oh, and I adored Tennessee Williams—I can't forget Tennessee Williams. He was a true poet of the human heart, and wrote parts for women like no one else did.

How about the classics?

Tolstoy, Chekhov, Pushkin, and Turgenev were all favorites of mine. Chekhov—he was another one who knew about women. I wanted to play Chekhov, God how I wanted to play Chekhov! Tolstoy, too—Anna Karenina would have been a stupendous role for any actress. I also read plays by Aristophanes, and works by Aristotle. I loved Proust and Flaubert, too. Flaubert had a cruel streak—did you know that? It's there in his writing, a kind of coldness for his own characters. But did you ever read *A Simple Heart*? Now that was wonderful. He really understood his character, and he made us understand her, too. And Proust—he never stopped longing for his mother's love and approval. I could certainly relate to that.

Did you like poetry? Did you ever try to write it yourself?

I did like reading poetry. Some of the poets I admired were Emily Dickinson, William Blake, A.E. Housman, and also some moderns, like E.E. Cummings, who could make me laugh out loud. Emily Dickinson was my favorite. Even though she barely went out of her house, she knew things, things that mattered, and she could write about them—God, death, love, the secret life of the soul. I tried my hand at poetry, but found I was no good. I would never show my poems to anyone.

THE BODY POLITIC

Marilyn did not concern herself overly with
politics. But when pressed, she could offer some
astute views. Even though she didn't have much
to say on the subject, her political leanings
were definitely toward the leftist camp. She
had a natural affinity for the downtrodden and
the underdog. Even though she may have been
attracted to powerful men on a personal level,
on a political level she did not identify with
those in power. She was not afraid to challenge
them either, putting her own popularity on the
line to support friends under pressure from
anti-communist witch-hunting in the 1950s.

*Did you consider yourself to be a person with strong
political views?*

I was not the most informed person politically, but I
was passionate. I had a strong sense of what I thought
was right, and I was disgusted by what I thought was
wrong—corruption, greed, intolerance, and stupidity.

Who did you vote for in the 1960 election?

Kennedy. I didn't trust Nixon, I thought he was shifty
and evil. I wanted no part of his world.

*You lived during a time of great social and political
upheaval in the United States, particularly in the arena
of civil rights. Can you comment on race relations as you
watched them being played out?*

I hated all the divisions there were between people, and in my own way I worked to eliminate them. Being a movie actress was a kind of democratic thing to do, because everyone—rich, poor, young, old, dark-skinned or light—loves movies. They appeal to everyone, because everyone needs a way to escape who they are, and movies can help you do that better than almost anything else. So I thought of myself as a kind of mascot for the masses.

Can you talk about what happened with Ella Fitzgerald? It's been said that she considers herself to be forever in your debt.

I didn't do anything so extraordinary when you think about it. She was the extraordinary one—that voice, my God, that voice! It just melted me. But back then, she was having trouble getting booked, can you believe it? Because of the color of her skin. When I got wind of this, I called the owner of the Mocambo in Hollywood, and told him that if he agreed to book Fitzgerald, I would take a front table every night. I knew that the press would go wild over this. So the owner booked her, and the press was even better than I'd hoped. Ella sang her heart out, night after night, and I was there to listen. After that, Ella didn't have any trouble getting bookings.

Part of the political drama you witnessed was the escalation of the Cold War between the United States and the Soviet Union, and you saw how America's fear of communism infiltrated Hollywood in significant ways. After Arthur Miller was questioned by the House Committee on Un-American Activities, you were urged to end your association with him. Can you talk about that experience?

Yes, some of those bastards in Hollywood wanted me to drop Arthur. They told me it would wreck my career. It was a terrible, even shattering thing. I was so ashamed of my country at that moment. And ashamed of a lot of my colleagues in the motion picture industry, too. They were cowards. But I didn't listen to any of them, and I'm glad. I never sold Arthur out, either. I can feel proud of that.

What about women's issues? Were you a feminist? Do you think there could ever be a woman president?

Feminist wasn't a word you heard much of back then. But yes, I suppose I was a feminist if that means believing that women are the equals of men, and should be given the same opportunities and respect. I fought for that in my own film career. People who typecast me as helpless sometimes forget that in the mid-50s I battled to get a contract that gave me control over the pictures I did and the directors I worked with. Do I think there could ever be a woman president? I don't know, but why not?

VISIONS OF HOME

Even at the height of her success, Monroe was a transient, a rolling stone who never became truly attached to any one place. Yet she longed for a home as much as she longed for love and security, and she tried to make a home for herself, whether through places, people, or even just a sense of being "at home" in her own skin. During her marriage to Arthur Miller they worked together on a country place in Connecticut. There, Frank Lloyd Wright made watercolor drawings for her of a dream house on a mountain top. But the dream remained a dream.

Were you emotionally attached to your home city of Los Angeles?

It's such an ugly town in so many ways that I once called it one big varicose vein. But ugly or not, I suppose I loved it because it was mine. That's how it is, you know? You can see all its faults, but still feel a certain tenderness toward it.

What about New York City? Could that have been home?

I loved New York, just flat out loved it. What an amazing town. And when I was with Arthur, I learned about Brooklyn Heights and I fell in love with that, too. I thought about buying a little house and living there most of the time. Just traveling back to the coast to make movies. To me, Brooklyn Heights felt both cosmopolitan and cozy at the same time. It was this wonderful neighborhood, with such a soul to it, and yet it was part of this great metropolis too—the best of both worlds.

What would your dream house be like?

It would have lots of windows, so you could look out in every direction. Big enough not to feel cluttered or cramped, but not too big either. Upstairs, there'd be a master bedroom for me, and a bathroom with a big tub and mirrors everywhere. A couple of guest rooms with their own bathrooms. Downstairs, a big kitchen, dining room, living room, and a little study, with a velvet-covered armchair and an antique writing desk, the sort of thing that Jane Austen might have used. I'd want the kinds of sofas and chairs you just sink down into. A few silk pillows, a cashmere throw. Persian rugs, because I love how they feel underfoot.

Lots of bookshelves, space for a few good paintings. A yard, with a cherry tree out back. Maybe an apple tree, too. I like apples. Plenty of room for animals, friends, lovers … a place that would make you want to come back again and again.

What did the idea of home mean for you?

Home was something I didn't know about from my own experience. I thought of it as a place that would give you a sense of continuity and enduring love. Robert Frost said home is the place that when you go there, they have to take you in. I never had that. But I never stopped trying to make a home, or stopped wishing for one either.

What about friendships? Did they provide you with a sense of being at home in the world?

It was hard to form friendships at the orphanage—most of the girls were so hurt and scared, they learned to be wary, not to trust other people. I always wished for friends, though. Especially a "best friend." I'd daydream about how we'd do things together—go to the movies, and then have an ice cream soda afterwards, sleep over at each other's houses, and stay up late doing each other's hair, giggling, and sharing all our secrets—stuff like that.

I did pal around with a few of the other girls at the Hollywood Club when I was first getting started in the business. But there was a lot of jealousy, backbiting, and petty gossip between us because we were all vying for the same parts, the same breaks. Not a lot of trust there. So I can't say I had any deep friendships in those years either, though I really wished I had.

CHILD OF MINE

Much has been written on the subject of
Marilyn and children—how she wanted them,
longed for them, and was deeply saddened,
even traumatized, by her failure to have them.
Yet the story is more complex than that, and
is inextricably laced with the story of her own,
damaged girlhood. When considering the
subject of Monroe and children, it has to be
remembered that the child she had been was
never far from the surface, and that it was the
continuing presence of that long-ago child—
abandoned, unwanted, unloved—that influenced
much of her thinking and her actions.

How much did you want to have children?

There's no simple answer to that. I always felt I
had a special connection with kids. When I was
married to Jim, I used to take care of his two young
nephews. I fed and bathed them, read them the
comics, played with them. But the thought of having
a baby then stood my hair on end. I could see it only
as myself, another Norma Jeane in an orphanage.
Something would happen to me. Jim would wander
off. And there'd be this little girl in the blue dress
and white blouse, living in her "aunt's" home,
washing dishes, being the last in the bath water on
Saturday night.

Did you try to have a child?

When I was young and on my own, no. I didn't want

to have a baby. I wasn't ready at that point. A child would have gotten in my way, prevented me from making my way up that tricky ladder of success I was so determined to climb. But I more than once got pregnant by accident. And so I had abortions, several of them, back in a time when having an abortion was a sordid, dirty thing done by doctors you wouldn't want to go to if you were sick. Even thinking of it now makes me shudder.

What was it like?

There was a doctor a lot of girls I knew used. He had an office above a funeral parlor—I'm not kidding—in a bad part of town. It was just two measly little rooms, and the guy just seemed so nervous. I remember that he wouldn't look you in the eye, ever, and that he was always sweating. Sweat beading his upper lip, sweaty

forehead, sweat staining the front of his grimy white
doctor's coat.

So you regret having had abortions?

I have conflicting thoughts about them. The
memories haunt me still—no woman should have to
go through something like that. But I wasn't capable
of caring for a child then, and it would have been
a worse sin to have had a child I couldn't care for.
I knew only too well what that was like, and how
it would play out. I couldn't have knowingly done
that to someone else. Abortion was a better, more
humane option.

*Nowadays there's a real division between pro-lifers and
women's right to choose. Which side would you take on
that fundamental issue?*

No one should tell another woman whether or not she should have a child. No one. Having an abortion may be a painful thing to go through, but every woman deserves the right to make the choice for herself. After all, she's the one who'll live with the consequences of her actions, whatever she chooses.

When did you first feel it was time for you to have children?

I loved Joe DiMaggio's children, and remained close to them even after we divorced. Yet I did begin to long for a child of my own when Joe and I parted. Maybe it was so I could repair the damage that had been done to me as a child. I wanted to rewrite the story, but this time, with a different ending.

I desperately wanted to have a child with Arthur Miller. He already had two children from his previous marriage, and I knew how much he loved them. I wanted him to love a child of ours in that complete, total, and unconditional way. So we tried. But it didn't work. I had miscarriages and an ectopic pregnancy. It's possible that the abortions I'd had did something to me inside, something bad, something that made it impossible for me to ever become pregnant in the normal way. I was anguished about it, you know. I mourned all those lost babies, every single last one of them.

If you'd been able to have children, would you have wanted a boy or a girl?

One of each! Or two, or three of each. Seriously. I never really cared about things like that, all those endless labels—boy or girl, handsome or pretty, athletic or smart. I just wanted someone I could love without any restraints or barriers at all. And someone who would return that love, in the pure, innocent way only a child can.

SANDS OF TIME

Marilyn died when she was only 36, well before she had really begun to age. Yet the issue of growing older was always on her mind. She was acutely aware of herself as a desirable, *young* actress and must have wondered what would become of her in a business where youth and beauty were prized above all else. Her illnesses and operations, combined with her heavy use of barbiturates and alcohol, inevitably took their toll. She was concerned about her age because she had to be: the world she lived in would never let her forget it.

Did it seem to you that Hollywood was a place for older women?

No, not really. Even great stars like Bette Davis, Joan Crawford, and Katharine Hepburn had trouble landing decent roles. What was offered them? Lunatics? Murderesses? The pickings were slim. It was disgusting. In Hollywood, you went from being a babe to a crone, with nothing in between. I would've loved to have seen that change.

Did you worry about your own aging process in the light of that?

Of course I did. How could I not worry about it? I didn't want to get old. I wanted to stay like I was. Because I was afraid that when my face went, and my body went, I'd be nothing—nothing—all over again. It was such a depressing thought, it used to get under my skin, like an itch or a rash. I'd have to fight to chase it away. Fight—or else drink a big glass of champagne.

How about with men? Did you fear that if your looks faded, you wouldn't be loved?

Yes, I worried about that, too, especially since men seemed to be so drawn to my physical assets. Yet I wanted to be a different sort of woman as far as men went, a woman like Simone Signoret, for instance. Simone never worried about Yves leaving her, even when he had affairs, which he did from time to time. But he was attached to her in a way that went much deeper than physical attraction. I always envied that connection and wished I could have it, too. But the men I was with seemed to value the surface above

all else. That was my curse, I suppose. Or one of
my curses.

Did you notice any signs of aging in yourself?
What did you think about having plastic surgery?

I had that very fine, white skin that is susceptible
to aging, and yes, I already saw a bit of deterioration,
especially around the eyes—tiny, tiny lines. But
I didn't want my face to be cut up and altered by
some surgeon. I wanted to have the courage to be
loyal to the face I'd made for myself.

What would you have done had you lived to be an
old woman? Would you have remained in Hollywood?
Or changed careers and direction?

I would have gone on being an actress, and fighting

for roles that I knew I deserved to get. Once I was finished as a sexpot, I'd have wanted to play strong, tough women, women of substance. And when I retired, I would have started raising dogs or horses or even both. I would have lived with animals, lots of them. I liked to fantasize about a modern-day version of Noah's Ark ... two of every kind.

MYSTERIES OF THE SOUL

Marilyn's inner world was one of yearning
and aspiration: there were so many things she
wanted to do and be. Part of the yearning she
felt was a spiritual one, and she passionately
longed for the kind of certainty and peace that
spiritual faith often provides. Part of her foster
childhood was spent with fundamentalists whose
slap-down severities put her off conventional
religion. Although she was not a devout person,
her yearning for some spiritual center, some
escape from a superficial existence, nevertheless
influenced the choices she made and the way
she lived her life.

Did you consider yourself a spiritual person?

Oh yes, very much so. I was always interested
in that deep, interior world, and the mystery of
the soul, which no one has ever really explained
or understood. But I believed in it as deeply as I
believed in anything. Why are we here? What is our
purpose on Earth? What joins us and what divides
us? Why are we each so different, like snowflakes
or fingerprints? To me, these kinds of spiritual
questions were always important, always intriguing.
Even when I was a child, I used to lie on my back
looking up at the sky and wondering about it all.

What was the religion with which you were raised?

I was raised as a kind of white-bread, watered-down
Christian. Mine was a religion of church suppers,

Sunday school, and psalm singing, but it was all kind of passionless. If you're going to be a Christian, at least be a Catholic. The Catholics have it over all the other Christians in terms of pageantry and drama.

What about your conversion to Judaism? Can you talk about why and how that happened?

Well, it came about through Arthur, of course. He was Jewish, and I wanted to be part of him, part of his family—whom I adored, by the way—and so it just felt right to me to become Jewish, too. I was officially converted on the morning of our marriage, by Rabbi Robert Goldberg, a friend of Arthur's who'd given me some instruction about the Jewish faith. I just loved the ideas he shared with me—the sanctity of the Sabbath, the spiritual and physical purity of the *mikvah*—these rituals spoke to something in my soul.

I used to joke that it was a shotgun conversion, but in fact it was no such thing. Neither Arthur nor his family ever pressured me to convert. It was my own idea from the start. They certainly supported me in it. But they didn't push. I felt comfortable being a Jew. I think I'd identified with Jews for a long time. Before I even met Arthur, I'd read his first novel, *Focus*, which was in part a study of how anti-Semitism affects identity and personality. Jews interested me because of their position as outsiders and their refusal to assimilate to the dominant culture. I, too, was an outsider, so I could relate to all this.

What about when you and Arthur split up? How did that affect your religious choices?

The divorce didn't change a thing. Even after Arthur and I split up, I remained Jewish. I felt embraced and accepted by this new faith. I didn't want to lose the connection. After all, I was already losing so much. When I first became a Jew, I was presented with a Certificate of Conversion. At the bottom were inscribed the words, *Thy people shall be my people, and thy God, my God*. That's from the Book of Ruth, and I always loved that line. I thought it was pure poetry. I kept the certificate, along with a brass-plated musical gold menorah that played the Israeli National Anthem. They were like talismans to me—things with magical properties to protect me and keep me safe. That's all I ever wanted, you know? To be protected and safe.

Did you think about sin a lot? Did you think suicide was a sin?

I did think about sin, but not in the conventional

way—I didn't think swearing or having sex or drinking was sinful. Hurting someone intentionally—that's a sin. Being cruel and relishing it—big sin. Suicide is not a sin. Suicide is the right of every suffering human soul.

What are your very last memories? Were you suffering so much that you wanted to take your own life?

I know this will sound strange, but I can't really answer that question. On a conscious level, the answer is no. I never took pills with the intent of ending my life. But I remember a night when I was in a terrible state. I was so lonely and frightened. Everything seemed to be falling apart—my work, my personal life. I didn't want to die. I wanted to end the pain, that's all. To be freed from it. I was agitated, and couldn't sleep, so I took some

Nembutal. I had a prescription for it and had been using it for some time.

The pills sent me to sleep but only for a while. After a few hours, I woke up again, even more frantic that I'd been before.

I tried making a phone call or two—I always loved talking on the phone late at night when I was unable to sleep, it was such a comforting thing to do—but I couldn't reach anyone. So I took some more pills. I don't remember how many, but it was quite a number—I had to drink a lot of water to wash them down. I didn't think about dying, though, I thought about sleeping. Shakespeare wrote, "Sleep, that knits up the raveled sleeve of care." That was me—the raveled sleeve of care. All I wanted was to be mended, healed, and made whole …

REFILL?

SELECTED BIBLIOGRAPHY

Georges Belmont, *Marilyn Monroe and the Camera* (New York: Little, Brown & Company, 1989)

James Haspiel, *Young Marilyn: Becoming the Legend* (New York: Hyperion, 1994)

Guss Luijters, *In Her Own Words: Marilyn Monroe* (London: Omnibus Press, 1990)

Norman Mailer, *Marilyn: A Biography* (New York: Grosset & Dunlap, 1973)

Arthur Miller and Serge Toubiana, *The Misfits: The Story of a Shoot* (London and New York: Phaidon, 2000)

Joyce Carol Oates, *Blonde* (New York: Ecco Press, 2000)

Gloria Steinem (photographs by George Barris), *Marilyn: Norma Jeane* (New York: Henry Holt, 1986)

The Personal Property of Marilyn Monroe, Exhibition Catalogue (New York: Christie's, 1999)

FILMOGRAPHY

July 17, 1946 Norma Jeane has her first audition with Ben Lyon at Twentieth Century Fox. In August of the same year, she is given her first studio contract with Fox and her name is changed to Marilyn Monroe.

Early 1947 Marilyn is given a bit part in *Scudda Hoo! Scudda Hay!* The film is shown in 1948, after the release of her second film, *Dangerous Years*.

1949 Marilyn appears in *Ladies of the Chorus*, playing the part of a burlesque queen, Peggy Martin.

Early 1949 Groucho Marx helps Marilyn land a small part in the Marx Brothers film *Love Happy*.

August 1949 In the Western *A Ticket to Tomahawk*, Marilyn takes on the role of Clara, a chorus girl.

January 1950 Shooting begins for *The Fireball*, with Marilyn cast as Polly, a roller-skating groupie.

1950 Marilyn appears in *Right Cross*, with June Allyson, Dick Powell, and Lionel Barrymore. She plays the part of Powell's girlfriend.

June 1950 John Huston gives Marilyn a more important role in *The Asphalt Jungle*. She plays Angela Phinlay, the young mistress of a corrupt politician.

Late 1950 Marilyn wins a seven-year contract with Twentieth Century Fox. She also has a memorable role as a starlet in the 1950 classic *All About Eve*, starring Bette Davis, Celeste Holm, and Anne Baxter.

1951 Marilyn plays the secretary Miss Martin in *Hometown Story*.

1951 Marilyn again appears as a secretary in *As Young as You Feel*.

April 1951 Shooting begins for *Love Nest*, in which Marilyn plays Roberta Stevens, an ex-member of the Women's Army Corps.

1951 Marilyn plays a gold-digger in *Let's Make It Legal*, which starred Claudette Colbert, Macdonald Carey, and Zachary Scott.

1952 Marilyn takes the role of Peggy, a fish cannery worker, in the drama *Clash by Night*.

1952 Marilyn is a beauty queen in *We're Not Married*, alongside Zsa Zsa Gabor.

1952 Acting against type, Marilyn plays a deranged babysitter in *Don't Bother to Knock*, which also stars Richard Widmark and Anne Bancroft.

1952 Marilyn plays yet another dumb blonde in Howard Hawks's *Monkey Business*.

1952 Marilyn lands the role of

a streetwalker in *O. Henry's Full House*, an adaptation of five short stories by O. Henry.

1952 Her first major role, as an unfaithful wife, comes in *Niagara*.

1953 Along with Jane Russell, she co-stars in the hit film *Gentlemen Prefer Blondes*, taking the coveted role of Lorelei Lee.

November 4, 1953 CinemaScope première of *How to Marry a Millionaire*, in which Marilyn and two friends (played by Lauren Bacall and Betty Grable) rent a posh apartment in the hope of snaring a trio of rich husbands. This highly successful film enhances Marilyn's reputation as a star.

Late 1953 Fox offers Marilyn $1,500 a week to co-star in *The Girl in Pink Tights* with Frank Sinatra, who is on $5,000 a week. She protests at this discrepancy and so is suspended.

1954 Marilyn, as a saloon singer, stars with Robert Mitchum in Otto Preminger's *River of No Return*.

1954 Acting alongside such legends as Ethel Merman, Donald O'Connor, Dan Dailey, and Mitzi Gaynor, Marilyn plays the part of Vicky, a nightclub singer in *There's No Business Like Show Business*.

August 1954 Filming begins for *The Seven Year Itch*. Directed by Billy Wilder, it tells the story of a married man's obsession with his lovely neighbor, played by Marilyn. Marilyn leaves Hollywood to study at the Actors Studio in New York before the film is released in 1955.

May 1956 After a year battling the Fox studio, Marilyn secures a new contract and stars in *Bus Stop*, directed by Joshua Logan.

July 14, 1956 Marilyn arrives in London to make *The Prince and the Showgirl*, her only independent production, which co-starred Sir

Laurence Olivier and was released in 1957.

1959 Marilyn co-stars with Tony Curtis and Jack Lemmon in Billy Wilder's *Some Like It Hot*, one of the most successful screen comedies ever made.

Early 1960 Marilyn begins filming *Let's Make Love*, directed by George Cukor and also starring Yves Montand.

July 18, 1960 Filming of *The Misfits* begins in Nevada. The film, written by Arthur Miller for Marilyn, is directed by John Huston. Marilyn shares the spotlight with her childhood idol, Clark Gable, and Montgomery Clift.

April 23, 1962 Marilyn begins work on *Something's Got to Give*, but her erratic behaviour brings filming to a halt and she is sued for breach of contract.

INDEX